Leisure

# GETTING TO KNOW THE WORLD'S GREATEST ARTISTS

## A N D Y
# WARHOL

### WRITTEN AND ILLUSTRATED BY MIKE VENEZIA

BROMLEY LIBRARIES

3 0128 02136 4685

D1585598

CHILDREN'S PRESS®
A DIVISION OF GROLIER PUBLISHING
NEW YORK   LONDON   HONG KONG   SYDNEY
DANBURY, CONNECTICUT

Cover: *Campbell's Soup I (Tomato),* by Andy Warhol. 1968.
One from portfolio of ten screenprints on white paper,
35 x 23 inches. © 1996 The Andy Warhol Foundation, Inc.

Project Editor: Shari Joffe
Design: Steve Marton
Photo Research: Jan Izzo

*The author would like to thank John Warhola
and the staff of the Andy Warhol Museum for their
valuable help with this book.*

**BROMLEY PUBLIC LIBRARIES**

| | |
|---|---|
| 021364685 | |
| Askews | 24.7.00 |
| J759 WAR | £5.99 |
| | CHL |

Library of Congress Cataloging–in–Publication Data

Venezia, Mike.
    Andy Warhol / written and illustrated by Mike Venezia.
       p. cm. — (Getting to know the world's greatest artists)
    Summary: A simple biography of a man who helped develop
Pop Art and made art fun for many people.
    ISBN 0-516-20053-4 (lib. bdg.) — ISBN 0-516-26075-8 (pbk.)
    1. Warhol, Andy, 1928 —Juvenile literature. 2. Artists-
United States—Biography—Juvenile literature
    [1. Warhol, Andy, 1928. 2. Artists.] I. Title. II. Series:
Venezia, Mike. Getting to know the world's greatest artists.
N6537.W28V46 1996
7700`.92—dc20
[B]
                     96-11725
                      CIP
                      AC

Copyright 1996 by Mike Venezia.
All rights reserved. Published simultaneously in Canada.
Printed in the United States of America.
    4 5 6 7 8 9 10 R 05 04 03 02 01 00 99

*Self-Portrait,* by Andy Warhol. 1966-67. Synthetic polymer paint and silkscreen on canvas, 22 x 22 inches. The Andy Warhol Museum, Pittsburgh Founding Collection, Contribution, The Andy Warhol Foundation for the Visual Arts, Inc., PO 40.074. Photo: Richard Stoner

Andy Warhol was born in Pittsburgh, Pennsylvania, in 1928. He helped develop Pop Art, one of the best-known and most fun periods of art ever. Andy Warhol also became one of the most famous artists ever. He may have been the first and only art superstar!

*Close Cover Before Striking (Pepsi Cola),* by Andy Warhol. 1962. Synthetic polymer paint and sandpaper on canvas, 72 x 54 inches. © 1996 The Andy Warhol Foundation, Inc.

Andy Warhol's best-known paintings and prints are usually brightly colored. They have simple, strong shapes that really stand out. Andy often showed things that were a popular part of everyday modern life, like supermarket products and rock stars. The name "Pop Art" comes from the word "popular."

*Elvis I and II,* by Andy Warhol. 1964. Panel 1: synthetic polymer paint and silkscreen ink on canvas. Panel 2: synthetic polymer paint and aluminum paint on canvas. Each: 82 x 82 inches. © 1996 The Andy Warhol Foundation, Inc.

When people first started seeing Pop Art, many of them were shocked. They couldn't believe that serious artists would make sculptures and pictures of such ordinary objects. But pop artists like Andy Warhol, Claes Oldenburg,

*Two Cheeseburgers, with Everything (Dual Hamburgers)*, by Claes Oldenburg. 1962. Burlap soaked in plaster, painted with enamel, 7 x 14 3/4 x 8 5/8 inches. The Museum of Modern Art, New York. Philip Johnson Fund. Photograph © 1996 The Museum of Modern Art, New York.

*Whaam!*, by Roy Lichtenstein. 1963. Magna on canvas. 2 panels;
68 x 166 inches total. © Roy Lichtenstein

and Roy Lichtenstein were just doing what artists have always done. They were creating art about things that were important or familiar in their everyday lives.

Andy Warhol had a natural talent for art. His mother encouraged him, and even helped him with his drawings when he was little. She was a pretty good artist, too.

At an early age, Andy started having some strange medical problems. First, he started feeling nervous and shaky a lot. Then, for some reason, he started to lose his skin color.

Andy was becoming paler all the time.
His mother insisted he spend a lot of
time resting in bed. Andy enjoyed taking
time out to rest. He colored, read his
favorite comic books, and listened to the
radio. He especially liked reading movie
magazines. Andy always loved movies.
He dreamed about the exciting and
glamorous lives of his favorite movie stars.

Andy showed so much interest in art at school that his teachers suggested he take weekend art classes at the nearby Carnegie Museum of Art. Andy met other talented kids there. Some of them were from rich families. For the first time, Andy saw how wealthy people lived. He imagined how nice it would be to have lots of money.

Even though Andy's family never had much money, Andy's father managed to save enough to send his son to art college. After Andy graduated from high school, he studied design and illustration at the Carnegie Institute of Technology.

While he was there, he developed an unusual art style. He drew his subject in pencil, and then went over the pencil lines in ink. Then, before the ink dried, Andy pressed his picture down onto a clean sheet of paper. This gave him a really neat blotted-line look.

*Untitled ("The Cat Resembled My Uncle Pierre"),* by Andy Warhol. c. 1954. Ink on paper, 16 x 13 1/2 inches. © 1996 The Andy Warhol Foundation, Inc.

After Andy graduated from art college, he went to New York City to look for a job. Because he had very little money, he carried his drawings and artwork around in a brown-paper grocery bag.

After showing his work to a lot of different advertising agencies and magazine publishers, Andy finally got lucky. An art director at *Glamour* magazine asked Andy to do some drawings of shoes to illustrate a story. Andy was thrilled! Not only was he going to make some money, but shoes were one of Andy's favorite things to draw.

Shoe illustration from *Glamour* magazine, by Andy Warhol. 1949. © Andy Warhol Foundation, Inc.

Later on, Andy did a whole series of ads for a big shoe store in New York, and even made some fun shoe drawings for himself. He kept using his blotted-line method, and everyone thought his illustrations were really original and great fun. His blotted-line art seemed to have an energy to it, almost like it was dancing around on the page. Andy kept getting more and more jobs, and before he knew it, he was making lots of money!

*A la Recherche du Shoe Perdu (Cover)*, by Andy Warhol. 1955.
Offset lithography, watercolor and pen on paper,
26 1/8 x 20 inches © 1996 The Andy Warhol Foundation, Inc.

Finally, Andy was able to move into a nice, big apartment. By this time, Andy's father had died, and his mother decided to move in with him. Andy was getting more work all the time. Not only was he doing magazine illustrations, but he started decorating department-store windows. He was also designing greeting cards, record albums, and book covers. He even drew suns, clouds, and raindrops for a television weather report.

Andy had so much work now that he sometimes asked his friends to help him finish things up. Andy's mom often did hand lettering for his illustrations. Andy was becoming one of the busiest—and wealthiest—illustrators in New York City!

*Cover From "In the Bottom of My Garden,"* by Andy Warhol. 1955. Ink and tempera on paper. 17 7/8 x 24 1/8 inches. © 1996 The Andy Warhol Foundation, Inc.

*Three Flags,* by Jasper Johns. 1958. Encaustic on canvas, 30 7/8 x 45 1/2 x 5 inches.
50th Anniversary Gift of the Gilman Foundation, Inc., The Lauder Foundation, A. Alfred
Taubman, an anonymous donor, and purchase. Collection of Whitney Museum of American
Art, New York. © 1996 Jasper Johns/Licensed by VAGA, New York, NY.

When he found time to relax, Andy often
went to movies and art galleries. During
this time, Andy saw the work of two artists
that really impressed him. Jasper Johns and
Robert Rauschenberg were doing new and
exciting things with painting and sculpture.

Both of these artists had also done department-store window displays like Andy, but now they were becoming famous for their more serious artwork. Andy Warhol decided it was time for him to become a serious artist too.

*Monogram,* by Robert Rauschenberg. 1955. Moderna Museet Stockholm. © 1996 Robert Rauschenberg/ Licensed by VAGA, New York, NY.

Even though Andy's dream of making lots of money was coming true, there was still something he wanted. More than anything else in the world, Andy wanted to be famous! Andy went to work right away. He made paintings of comic-strip characters, newspaper ads, and supermarket products. Andy was looking for a way to make his art different from anyone else's, but he wasn't getting anywhere. No one seemed at all interested in Andy's paintings.

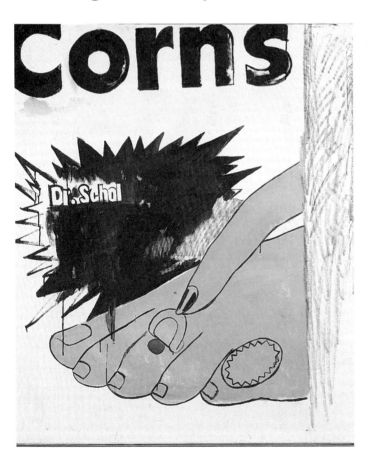

*Dr. Scholl*, by Andy Warhol. 1960. Oil on canvas, 40 x 48 inches. The Metropolitan Museum of Art, Gift of Halston, 1982 (1982.505).

*Superman*, by Andy Warhol. 1960. Synthetic polymer paint and crayon on canvas, 67 x 52 inches. © 1996 The Andy Warhol Foundation, Inc.

Andy started getting nervous about what to do. Finally, a friend told him she knew exactly what to do, but it would cost Andy $50 to find out.

Andy gladly paid his friend. She told him that since he loved money so much, he should paint money. For the same $50, she added another idea—to paint something he saw every day, like a can of Campbell's soup.  Andy thought his friend's ideas were great. Right away, he started painting pictures of money and soup cans.

Andy Warhol often asked people for ideas. He thought it was a normal part of creating things. Andy always made sure, though, that the way he showed those ideas was original and all his own.

*Campbell's Soup I (Tomato)*, by Andy Warhol. 1968. One from portfolio of ten screenprints on white paper, 35 x 23 inches. © 1996 The Andy Warhol Foundation, Inc.

*One Hundred Cans,* by Andy Warhol. 1962. Synthetic polymer paint on canvas, 72 x 52 inches. Collection Albright-Knox Art Gallery, Buffalo, New York, Gift of Seymour H. Knox, 1963. © 1996 The Andy Warhol Foundation, Inc.

Andy worked as hard as he could. He painted his soup cans on blank backgrounds to make them stand out and seem very important. Andy tried to make his paintings of money and canned soup look like they were printed or made by a machine—the way they were made in real life. He thought repeated images were an important part of Pop Art, too, because things are repeated in real life all the time. It's kind of like when you see the same TV commercials all the time or the same ads and billboards popping up. TV news shows and newspapers often repeat the same story over and over again, too.

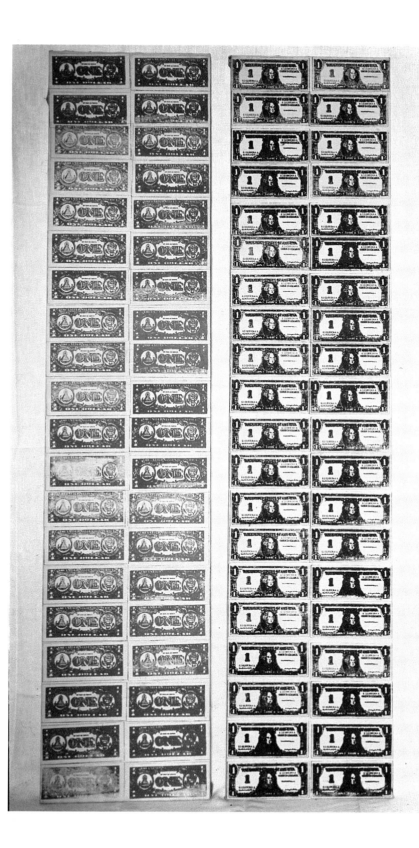

*Front and Back Dollar Bills,*
by Andy Warhol. 1962. Silkscreen
ink on canvas, two panels,
each 83 x 19 inches. Collection
Jed Johnson. © 1996 The Andy
Warhol Foundation, Inc.

Photo of Andy Warhol working at the Factory, by Billy Name.
Photo © Billy Name.

Andy Warhol's paintings finally started catching on. People enjoyed the fun, bright colors and pictures of things that were familiar to them. Andy was so busy, he not only had to get help from his mother and friends, he also had to hire assistants. They all worked in a big studio that Andy called the Factory.

Andy started using a way to print his paintings called photo silk-screening. Now he and his helpers could make hundreds of copies of each painting. Sometimes Andy gave unclear directions to his assistants. He wanted to see if they would come up with interesting surprises.

# Andy Warhol went on to make paintings and prints of all kinds of popular subjects.

*Do It Yourself (Flowers)*, by Andy Warhol. 1962. Synthetic polymer paint, Prestype and pencil on canvas, 69 x 59 inches. Private Collection. © The Andy Warhol Foundation, Inc.

Top left: *Tuna Disaster,* by Andy Warhol. 1963.
Silkscreen ink and aluminum paint on canvas,
41 x 22 inches. © 1995 The Andy Warhol
Foundation, Inc.

Top right: *Shot Red Marilyn,* by Andy Warhol. 1964.
Synthetic polymer paint and silkscreen ink on
canvas, 40 x 40 inches. © 1996 The Andy Warhol
Foundation, Inc.

Right: *Cow,* by Andy Warhol. 1966. Screenprint
printed on wallpaper, 45 1/2 x 29 3/4 inches.
© 1996 The Andy Warhol Foundation, Inc.

For a while, Andy stopped painting, and started making movies of everyday events, like *Sleep*, which showed a man sleeping for six hours. *Empire* showed the same view of the Empire State Building for eight hours, and *Eat* showed a man eating a mushroom for forty-five minutes. Andy's movies got a lot of attention, and are considered an important part of art and film history.

Stills from the film *Empire*, by Andy Warhol. 1964.
© 1994 The Andy Warhol Foundation for the Visual Arts, Inc.

Andy Warhol's life was filled with excitement. He was always in the news for one reason or another. By the time he died in 1987, he was a wealthy and famous artist, just what he had always hoped to be.

*Self Portrait,* by Andy Warhol. 1986. Synthetic polymer paint and silkscreen ink on canvas, 80 x 80 inches.
© 1996 The Andy Warhol Foundation, Inc.

*Myths: Mickey Mouse,* by Andy Warhol. 1981. Synthetic polymer paint and silkscreen ink on canvas, 60 x 60 inches. © 1996 The Andy Warhol Foundation, Inc.

Andy Warhol's Pop Art was really more than just a series of fun pictures of popular subjects. His best paintings and prints were beautifully designed. They are strong and powerful images with great colors. Andy's artwork and films made many people take a look around them and think about what really was and wasn't important in their lives.

**The works of art in this book are from the following places:**

The Andy Warhol Foundation, Inc., New York, New York

The Andy Warhol Museum, Pittsburgh, Pennsylvania

The Museum of Modern Art, New York, New York

Whitney Museum of American Art, New York, New York

Visual Artists and Galleries Association, Inc., New York, New York

The Metropolitan Museum of Art, New York, New York

Albright-Knox Art Gallery, Buffalo, New York